THE
WAY
TO
WEALTH

BENJAMIN FRANKLIN.
1706–1790

THE
WAY
TO
WEALTH

Benjamin Franklin

Applewood Books

ISBN: 0-918222-88-5

The Way to Wealth was first published in 1758 as a preface to Benjamin Franklin's *Poor Richard's Almanack*. In this preface, Franklin summed up all of his previously published thoughts about how to achieve success in business. For this purpose, Franklin created Father Abraham, who liberally quotes from Poor Richard to a crowd waiting for an auction to begin. The essay has become one of the most important and enduring business books ever published. It has been printed and reprinted almost 400 times and has been translated into almost every language. We are delighted to present it here, still as true today as when it was first printed. ❧

COURTEOUS READER,

I HAVE heard, that nothing gives an author so great pleasure, as to find his works respectfully quoted by others. Judge, then, how much I must have been gratified by an incident I am going to relate to you. I stopped my horse, lately, where a great number of people were collected at an auction of merchant's goods. The hour of the sale not being come, they were conversing on the badness of the times; and one of the company called to a plain, clean, old man, with white locks, "pray, father Abraham, what think you of the times? Will not those heavy taxes quite ruin the

Poor Richard stops at an auction

An elder named Father Abraham is asked by the crowd to speak on taxes

country? How shall we ever be able to pay them? What would you advise us to do?"—Father Abraham stood up, and replied, "If you would have my advice, I will give it you in short; 'for a word to the wise is enough,' as Poor Richard says." They joined in desiring him to speak his mind, and gathering round him, he proceeded as follows: 🙤 " 'Friends,' says he, 'the taxes are, indeed, very heavy; and, if those laid on by the government were the only ones we had to pay, we might more easily discharge them; but we have many others, and much more grievous to some of us. We are taxed twice as much by our idleness, three times as much by our pride, and four times as much by our folly; and from these taxes the commissioners can-

Father Abraham stands up and begins quoting Poor Richard

We are taxed twice as much by our idleness, three times as much by our pride, and four times as much by our folly

not ease or deliver us, by allowing an abatement. However, let us hearken to good advice and something may be done for us; 'God helps them that helps themselves,' as Poor Richard says.

God helps those who help themselves

I "It would be thought a hard government that should tax its people one tenth part of their time, to be employed in its service: But idleness taxes many of us much more; sloth, by bringing on diseases, absolutely shortens life. 'Sloth, like rust, consumes faster than labour wears, while the used key is always bright,' as Poor Richard says.—'But dost thou love life, then do not squander time, for that is the stuff life is made of,' as Poor Richard says.—How much more than is necessary do we spend in

INDUSTRY

If you love life, then do not squander time, for that is the stuff life is made of

The sleeping fox catches no poultry

sleep! forgetting that 'The sleeping fox catches no poultry, and that there will be sleeping enough in the grave,' as Poor Richard says.

🔔 " 'If time be of all things the most precious, wasting time must be,' as Poor Richard says, 'the greatest prodigality'; since, as he elsewhere tells us, 'Lost time is never found again; and what we call time enough always proves little enough': Let us then up and be doing, and doing to the purpose: So by diligence shall we do more with less perplexity. 'Sloth makes all things difficult, but industry all easy; and, he that riseth late, must trot all day, and shall scarce overtake his business at night; while Laziness travels so slowly, that Poverty soon overtakes him. Drive thy business, let not that drive thee;

Lost time is never found again

He who rises late must trot all day

and early to bed, and early to rise, makes a man healthy, wealthy, and wise,' as Poor Richard says. 🐚 "So what signifies wishing and hoping for better times? We may make these times better, if we bestir ourselves. 'Industry need not wish, and he who lives upon hope will die fasting. There are no gains without pains; then help hands, for I have no lands,' or, if I have, they are smartly taxed. 'He that hath a trade, hath an estate; and he that hath a calling, hath an office of profit and honour,' as Poor Richard says; but then the trade must be worked at, and the calling well followed, or neither the estate nor the office will enable us to pay our taxes.—If we are industrious we shall never starve; for, 'at the working man's house hunger looks in,

Early to bed and early to rise, makes a man healthy, wealthy, and wise

There are no gains without pains

At the working man's house, hunger looks in, but dares not enter

but dares not enter.' Nor will the bailiff or the constable enter, for 'Industry pays debts, while despair increaseth them.' What though you have found no treasure, nor has any rich relation left you a legacy, 'Diligence is the mother of good luck, and God gives all things to industry. Then plough deep, while sluggards sleep, and you shall have corn to sell and keep.' Work while it is called today, for you know not how much you may be hindered tomorrow. 'One today is worth two tomorrows,' as Poor Richard says; and farther, 'Never leave that till tomorrow, which you can do today.' — If you were a servant, would you not be ashamed that a good master should catch you idle? Are you then your own master? Be ashamed to catch yourself idle

Industry pays debts, while despair increases them

Plough deep, while sluggards sleep, and you shall have corn to sell and keep

Never leave till tomorrow what you can do today

when there is so much to be done for yourself, your family, your country, and your king. Handle your tools without mittens: Remember, that 'The cat in gloves catches no mice,' as Poor Richard says. It is true, there is much to be done, and perhaps, you are weak handed; but stick to it steadily, and you will see great effects; for 'Constant dropping wears away stones; and by diligence and patience the mouse ate in two the cable; and little strokes fell great oaks.' 🐚 "Methinks I hear some of you say, 'Must a man afford himself no leisure?' I will tell thee, my friend, what Poor Richard says; 'Employ thy time well, if thou meanest to gain leisure; and, since thou are not sure of a minute, throw not away an hour.' Leisure is the time for

The cat in gloves catches no mice

Little strokes fell great oaks

Since you are not sure of a minute, do not throw away an hour

doing something useful; this leisure the diligent man will obtain, but the lazy man never; for, 'A life of leisure and a life of laziness are two things. Many, without labour, would live by their wits only, but they break for want of stock;' whereas industry gives comfort, and plenty, and respect. 'Fly pleasures, and they will follow you. The diligent spinner has a large shift; and now I have a sheep and a cow every body bids me good morrow.'

A life of leisure and a life of laziness are two different things

CARE II "But with our industry we must likewise be steady, settled, and careful, and oversee our own affairs with our own eyes, and not trust too much to others; for, as Poor Richard says,

'I never saw an oft removed tree,
Nor yet and oft removed family,
That throve so well as those that settled be.'

"And again, 'Three removes are as bad as a fire:' And again, 'Keep thy shop, and thy shop will keep thee:' And again, 'If you would have your business done, go; if not, send.' And again,

Keep your shop and your shop will keep you

'He that by the plough would thrive,
Himself must either hold or drive.'

"And again, 'The eye of the master will do more work than both his hands:' And again, 'Want of care does more damage than want of knowledge:' And again, 'Not to oversee workmen is to leave them your purse open.' Trusting too much to other's care is the ruin of many; for, 'In the affairs of this world, men are saved, not by faith, but by the want of it:' But a man's own care is profitable; for, 'If you would have a faithful servant and one that you like — serve yourself.

The eye of the master will do more work than both his hands

If you want a faithful servant, and one that you like — serve yourself

A little neglect may breed great mischief; for want of a nail the shoe was lost; for want of a shoe the horse was lost; and for want of a horse the rider was lost, being overtaken and slain by the enemy; all for want of a little care about a horse shoe nail.

FRUGALITY III "So much for industry, my friends, and attention to one's own business; but to these we must add frugality, if we would make our industry more certainly successful. A man may, if he knows not how to save as he gets, 'keep his nose all his life to the grindstone, and die not worth a groat at last. A fat kitchen maketh a lean will;' and

A fat kitchen makes a lean will

'Many estates are spent in the getting,
Since women for tea forsook spinning and
      knitting,
And men for punch forsook hewing and
      splitting.'

'If you would be wealthy, think of saving, as well as of getting. The Indies have not made Spain rich, because her outgoes are greater than her incomes.' 🐚 "Away, then, with your expensive follies, and you will not have then so much reason to complain of hard times, heavy taxes, and chargeable families; for

'Women and wine, game and deceit,
Make the wealth small, and the want great.'

"And farther, 'What maintains one vice, would bring up two children.' You may think, perhaps, that a little tea or a little punch now and then, diet a little more costly, clothes a little finer, and a little entertainment now and then, can be no great matter; but remember, 'Many a little makes a mickle.' Beware of little expenses; 'A small leak

If you want to be wealthy, think of saving, as well as of earning

What maintains one vice would bring up two children

Beware of little expenses; A small leak will sink a great ship

will sink a great ship,' as Poor Richard says; and again, 'Who dainties love, shall beggars prove;' and moreover, 'Fools make feasts, and wise men eat them.' Here you are all got together at this sale of fineries, and knickknacks. You call them goods; but, if you do not take care, they will prove evils to some of you. You expect they will be sold cheap, and, perhaps, they may [be bought] for less than they cost; but, if you have no occasion for them, they must be dear to you. Remember what Poor Richard says, 'Buy what thou hast no need of, and ere long thou shalt sell thy necessaries.' And again, 'At a great penny worth pause a while:' He means, that perhaps the cheapest is apparent only, and not real; or the bargain, by straightening thee in

Fools make feasts, and wise men eat them

Buy what you do not need, and soon you will sell your necessities

thy business, may do thee more harm than good. For in another place he says, 'Many have been ruined by buying good penny worths.' Again, 'It is foolish to lay out money in a purchase of repentance;' and yet this folly is practised every day at auctions, for want of minding the Almanack. Many a one, for the sake of finery on the back, have gone with a hungry belly, and half starved their families; 'Silks and satins, scarlets and velvets, put out the kitchen fire,' as Poor Richard says. These are not the necessaries of life; they can scarcely be called the conveniences: And yet only because they look pretty, how many want to have them?—By these, and other extravagancies, the genteel are reduced to poverty, and forced to

It is foolish to lay out money in a purchase of repentance

Silks and satins and scarlets and velvets put out the kitchen fire

borrow of those whom they formerly despised, but who, through industry and frugality, have maintained their standing; in which case it appears plainly, that 'A ploughman on his legs is higher than a gentleman on his knees,' as Poor Richard says. Perhaps they have had a small estate left them, which they knew not the getting of; they think 'It is day, and never will be night;' that a little to be spent out of so much is not worth minding; but 'Always taking out of the meal tub, and never putting in, soon comes to the bottom,' as Poor Richard says; and then, 'When the well is dry, they know the worth of water.' But this they might have known before, if they had taken this advice. 'If you would know the value of money, go and try to bor-

A ploughman on his legs is higher than a gentleman on his knees

Always taking out of the pot, and never putting in, one soon comes to the bottom

If you want to know the value of money, go and try to borrow some

row some; for he that goes a bor-
rowing, goes a sorrowing,' as Poor
Richard says; and, indeed, so does
he that lends to such people, when
he goes to get it again. Poor Dick
farther advises, and says,

'Fond pride of dress is sure a very curse,
Ere fancy you consult, consult your purse.'

"And again, 'Pride is as loud a beggar as want, and a great deal more
saucy.' When you have bought one
fine thing, you must buy ten more,
that your appearance may be all of
a piece; but Poor Dick says, 'It is
easier to suppress the first desire,
than to satisfy all that follow it.'
And it is as truly folly for the poor
to ape the rich, as for the frog to
swell, in order to equal the ox.

Pride is as loud a beggar as need

It is easier to suppress the first desire than to satisfy all that follow it

'Vessels large may venture more,
But little boats should keep near shore.'

"It is, however, a folly soon punished; for, as Poor Richard says, 'Pride that dines on vanity, sups on contempt; Pride breakfasted with Plenty, dined with Poverty, and supped with Infamy.' And, after all, of what use is this pride of appearance, for which so much is suffered? It cannot promote health, nor ease pain; it makes no increase of merit in the person, it creates envy, it hastens misfortune. &⸱ "But what madness it must be to run in debt for these superfluities? We are offered, by the terms of this sale, six months credit; and that, perhaps, has induced some of us to attend it, because we cannot spare the ready money, and hope now to be fine without it. But ah! think what you do when you run into debt; you give to another power over your

Pride that dines on vanity sups on contempt

Think what you do when you run into debt

liberty. If you cannot pay on time, you will be ashamed to see your creditor; you will be in fear when you speak to him; you will make poor pitiful sneaking excuses, and by degrees, come to lose your veracity, and sink into base downright lying; for 'The second vice is lying the first is running in debt,' as Poor Richard says; and again, to the same purpose, 'Lying rides upon Debt's back:' Whereas a free born Englishman ought not to be ashamed nor afraid to see or speak to any man living. But poverty often deprives a man of all spirit and virtue. 'It is hard for an empty bag to stand upright.' What would you think of that prince, or of that government, who should issue an edict forbidding you to dress like a gentleman or gentlewoman, on

The second vice is lying, the first is running into debt

It is hard for an empty bag to stand upright

pain of imprisonment or servitude? Would you not say you were free, have a right to dress as you please, and that such an edict would be a breach to your privileges, and such a government tyrannical? and yet you are about to put yourself under that tyranny, when you run in debt for such dress! Your creditor has authority, at his pleasure, to deprive you of your liberty, by confining you in gaol for life, or by selling you for a servant, if you should not be able to pay him. When you have got your bargain, you may, perhaps, think a little of payment; *Creditors have* but, as Poor Richard says, 'Credi- *better memories* tors have better memories than *than debtors* debtors; creditors are a superstitious sect, great observers of set days and times.' The day comes round before you are aware, and the demand is made before you are able to satisfy it; or, if you bear your debt in mind, the term which at first seemed so long, will, as it lessens, appear extremely short: Time will seem to have added wings to his heels as well as his shoulders. 'Those have a short lent, who owe money to be paid at Easter.' At present, perhaps, you may think yourselves in thriving circumstances; and that you can bear a little extravagance without injury; but

Those have a short Lent, who owe money to be paid by Easter

'For age and want save while you may,
No morning sun lasts a whole day.'

"Gain may be temporary and uncertain, but ever, while you live, expense is constant and certain; and, 'It is casier to build two chimnies, than to keep one in fuel,' as Poor Richard says: So, 'Rather go to bed

Rather go to bed supperless, than rise in debt

supperless, than rise in debt

Get what you can, and what you get hold,
'Tis the stone that will turn all your lead into
gold.'

"And when you have got the philosopher's stone, sure you will no longer complain of bad times, or the difficulty of paying taxes.

IV "This doctrine, my friends, is reason and wisdom: But, after all, do not depend too much upon your own industry and frugality, and prudence, though excellent things; for they may all be blasted without the blessing of heaven; and therefore, ask the blessing humbly, and be not uncharitable to those that at present seem to want it, but comfort and help them. Remember Job suffered and was afterwards prosperous. ಶ "And now to conclude, 'Experience keeps a dear

Experience keeps an expensive school, but fools will learn in no other

school, but fools will learn in no other,' as Poor Richard says, and scarce in that; for it is true, 'We may give advice, but we cannot give conduct.' However, remember this, 'They that will not be coun- selled, cannot be helped;' and far- ther, that 'If you will not hear Reason, she will surely rap your knuckles,' as Poor Richard says." ❧ Thus the old gentleman ended his harangue. The people heard it, and approved the doc- trine, and immediately practiced the contrary, just as if it had been a common sermon; for the auction opened, and they began to buy ex- travagantly. I found the good man had thoroughly studied my Alma- nack, and digested all I had dropt on these topicks during the course of 25 years. The frequent mention

Those who will not be counselled, cannot be helped

he made of me must have tired any one else; but my vanity was wonderfully delighted with it, though I was conscious, that not a tenth part of the wisdom was my own, which he ascribed to me; but rather the gleanings that I had made of the sense of all ages and nations. However, I resolved to be the better for the echo of it; and though I had at first determined to buy stuff for a new coat, I went away, resolved to wear my old one a little longer. Reader, if thou wilt do the same, thy profit will be as great as mine. I am, as ever, thine to serve thee,

Poor Richard, upon hearing his own words echoed by Father Abraham, resolves to wear his old coat a little longer

&. RICHARD SAUNDERS